I love
Gymnastics

DK

LONDON, NEW YORK, MUNICH,
MELBOURNE, AND DELHI

Designer & Brand Manager Lisa Lanzarini
Project Editor Amy Junor
Consultant Vincent Walduck
Publishing Managers Cynthia O'Neill Collins
and Simon Beecroft
Art Director Mark Richards
Category Publisher Alex Allan
Production Ian Sherratt

First American Edition, 2005

Published in the United States by
DK Publishing, Inc.
375 Hudson Street
New York, New York 10014

06 07 08 09 10 9 8 7 6 5 4 3 2

A Cataloging-in-Publication record for this book is available
from the Library of Congress.

ISBN 0-7566-1011-7

Reproduced by Media Development and Printing, Ltd.
Printed and bound at Tlaciarne BB, Slovakia

Discover more at
www.dk.com

*These exercises and positions
should only be attempted under
the supervision of a qualified
gymnastics teacher.*

I love Gymnastics

Written *by* Naia Bray-Moffatt
Photography *by* David Handley

Contents

Introduction 7

Getting Started 8-9

Stretching 10-11

The Splits 12-13

Conditioning 14-15

Forward and Backward Rolls 16-17

Headstands and Handstands 18-19

The Cartwheel 20-21

Jumping and Leaping 22-23

Vaulting 24-25

Balancing on the Beam 26-27

Asymmetric Bars 28-29

Moving Up 30-31

Floor Sequence 32-33

Advanced Beam 34-35

Boys' Apparatus 36-37

Rings and Bars 38-39

Preparing for the Championship 40-41

Championship 42-43

Olympic Dreams 44-45

Glossary and Index 46-47

Acknowledgments 48

Introduction

Gymnastics teaches us how to move and control our bodies in special ways. You will learn to balance on a beam, swing on the bars, and roll on the floor. For girls and boys, gymnastics is a great way to make your body stronger and more flexible. It's great fun, too!

Getting Started

In the changing rooms, Jessica and Hannah put on their gymnastics club leotards. Jessica helps Hannah tie her hair back to stop it from falling in her eyes and so she looks neat and tidy.

Jessica loved gymnastics at school, so she joined a gymnastics club to learn more. Now Jessica does gymnastics twice a week and really enjoys all the new skills she is learning. The club has lots of classes for girls and boys of all ages and abilities. Today, Jessica has brought her friend Hannah who is looking forward to her first lesson at the club.

Jessica takes Hannah to meet their coach, Sarah. It is Sarah's job to teach the children to perform new gymnastic skills correctly and safely.

Warming up

Every lesson begins with a warm-up routine to prepare the body for the special exercises you will be doing. Running, jumping, and hopping make your heart beat faster. This increases your blood supply, giving you more energy and warming up your muscles.

Running

The spider walk

High jumps

Look how high Jessica and Hannah can jump! Tucking their knees makes their jump look even higher.

The girls run in a circle 10 times before changing direction and running the other way.

Creeping along the floor on your hands and feet like a spider is a good warm-up exercise. Don't forget to keep your head up so you can see where you're going!

"Hopping races are a lot of fun!"
Hannah

A *spring in your step*

The floor area of the gym is specially sprung and covered with carpet to give it bounce. It helps the gymnasts perform their exercises more easily and safely. It makes hopping easier, too!

One of the very first things the class learns is how to stand properly. Good posture will make all their movements look more elegant.

Sideways stretch

The class begins with some exercises to stretch their arms and upper body. They stretch one arm over their head as far as they can. After holding this stretch for a few moments, they do the same thing leaning over to the other side.

Stretching

After the energetic warm-up routine, the class have a chance to get their breath back with some stretching exercises. These are done slowly and each one is designed to stretch a different part of your body to help make you more flexible. Try and stretch as far as you can, but take care not to over-stretch your muscles because this will strain them. As you become more flexible, you will find that you can stretch even further.

Arm circles

Hannah pretends she is brushing her ears with her arms as she starts her arm circle movement. Jessica turns her shoulders to move her arms behind her back.

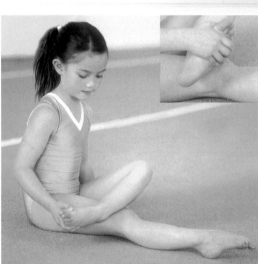

Putting your feet up

Hannah sits down but she isn't really resting. She is circling her feet because she knows that gymnasts need strong and flexible ankles and feet.

Full stretch

Molly is now warmed up so she can easily hold her leg up in this Y-balance without fear of damaging her muscles.

Floor stretches

Tyra concentrates on keeping her legs straight and flat on the floor as she bends forward in the lumberfold to touch her toes. This also stretches her hamstrings, which are tendons at the back of the knee.

Flat out

Tyra and Tiggy see if they can make their bellies touch the floor while they stretch their arms out in front of them and move their legs out to the side in the japana position.

Clasping your hands together and moving the wrists up and down is great for stretching and strengthening your wrists.

Straddle lever

It's a good thing Jessica has been practicing her hand exercises! She needs strong wrists to support her body weight in this position called the straddle lever.

Back stretch

Tiggy is stretching her lower back. Using her hands to support her weight, she lifts her upper body, while her legs are stretched out behind. She pushes back her shoulders and arches her back.

Flexibility

Learning how to do the splits will help you become more supple and flexible. Don't worry if you can't do the splits straight away. You will become more flexible with practice.

The Splits

One of the most important stretches you learn in gymnastics is the splits. There are two ways of doing the splits. In the front splits, the gymnast stretches one leg in front and one leg behind her. In the box splits, she stretches her legs out to the sides. You will probably find one way easier to do than the other.

Forward lunge

Full front splits

Jessica and Tyra show Hannah how they learned the front splits. They begin with the forward lunge, bending one leg and stretching the other leg behind them.

After practicing the forward lunge, Jessica and Tyra are now ready to push themselves all the way down into the full front splits.

Stretched toes

In most gymnastic moves, including both splits, it is important to keep your toes stretched. Hannah has lovely stretched toes.

" *I'm going to keep on trying!* "
Hannah

Half box splits

Hannah is learning to do the box splits. She bends her left knee out to the side, then stretches her right leg out to the other side and tries to get down as low as she can without straining.

Remember to keep your body facing forward, your back straight, and your head looking up.

Jessica is naturally flexible and can do the box splits as well as the front splits.

Full box splits with side bend

To do the box splits, start with the half splits that Hannah has just learned. Each time you practice, you will find you can get a little lower down to the floor. Then you can straighten your other leg out to the side. When you can do this, try bending over and touching your toes, like Jessica.

Half box splits

Conditioning

As well as being supple, gymnasts need to be strong. Gymnasts do strengthening exercises to condition their bodies, prepare them for the gymnastic skills they will perform, and to help them learn new skills more quickly. Most conditioning exercises have to be repeated several times to strengthen the muscles properly.

Wall bars
Hanging from the wall bars, Hannah must lift her legs slowly up and down 10 times.

Rope climbing
Jessica helps Molly hold the rope straight for Hannah and watches her use her feet and arms to push her way to the top.

Dish

The girls lie down on their backs and slowly raise their head, arms, and legs off the floor to make a dish shape. Molly pushes the lower part of her back into the floor, but it's hard to remember to keep your hands and legs together at the same time.

Arch

Next the girls turn over onto their bellies to make an arch shape. This time, they must curve, or arch, their backs to help lift their arms and legs off the floor.

Front support

Tyra tries to keep her body in a straight line as she practices the front support position. At first her hands should be in line with her shoulders, then she walks her arms out forward as far as she can and holds the position for 10 seconds. Well done Tyra!

Bridge

Tiggy can now make a good bridge and shows Hannah what the shape should look like. Tiggy's back is beautifully arched, her arms are straight and her legs slope downwards in a straight line.

Hannah tries to make a bridge shape. She lies on her back with her knees and arms bent and hands and feet on the floor. From this position, she pushes her body up to make the bridge.

Forward and Backward Rolls

One of the first skills you learn as a baby, even before you can walk, is how to roll—from your belly onto your back and from side to side. In gymnastics you will learn how to roll in many different ways and on all the pieces of apparatus. It's a lot of fun and an important skill. The two basic rolls are the forward and backward rolls. Today, the class are practicing how to do both of these rolls in a controlled way so that the movement is smooth and balanced, and with a tightly formed shape.

1 Jessica begins her forward roll standing up straight with her arms in the air.

Squat position

Head down

Tuck

Roll

2 She bends her knees and moves onto the balls of her feet in the squat position, with her arms out in front.

3 To start the roll, Jessica places both hands flat on the floor and tucks her head down before pushing off strongly and evenly with her legs.

4 Jessica keeps her chin close to her chest and her knees tightly bent to help her stay in the tucked position as she is rolling.

5 Reaching forward with her arms, Jessica comes out of the roll. The speed of the roll helps Jessica back into the squat position.

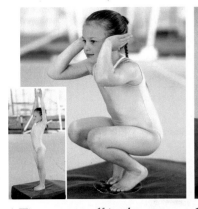

Tiggy is learning the backward roll. This is a bit harder than the forward roll because you need more strength in your arms to push your body backward over your head. To help her, Tiggy uses a sloping foam springboard.

1 *Tiggy starts off in the squat position at the top of the slope and puts her hands, palms facing up, by her ears.*

2 *She rolls down backward onto her hands. She must push strongly with her hands to lift her legs up and over her head.*

3 *Tiggy finishes on the floor back in the squat position. Now she must try without using the slope.*

Straight legs

Molly has learned how to do the forward roll in a tucked position, like Jessica. Now she is practicing a forward roll in a piked position, starting with straight legs and finishing with her legs apart in the straddle position, standing up.

Jessica and Hannah have gained confidence in their rolling and enjoy the fast-moving action forward roll.

Supported headstand

The chalk triangle on the floor shows Tyra where to position her head and hands. She puts the front of her head down at the top of the triangle where she will be balancing—not the top of her head.

Both positions need practice and, to begin with, the girls help support each other until they feel confident enough to do the skill on their own.

Headstands and Handstands

Today the class is turning themselves upside down and learning to balance on their head and hands. The children start with the headstand, which is easier because you have your head to balance on as well as your hands. Then they practice the handstand. This is the most important of all the skills you learn in gymnastics. The class concentrate hard on learning it correctly.

Walk your feet in

Bend and lift your legs

Straighten your legs

1 With legs straight, Tyra walks her feet in toward her hands. Molly stands safely to one side to make sure she doesn't get kicked.

2 Tyra lifts her legs and bends them into a tucked position. With Molly supporting Tyra around the waist, Tyra brings her hips over head.

3 Now Tyra lifts her legs until they are up above her head. Her legs are slightly tilted so that her weight is evenly distributed between her hands and her head.

At first, Jessica feels more comfortable with Tyra supporting her handstand.

Tucked headstand

Molly gets down on all fours to act as a wall to support Tyra and stop her from falling over as she practices a headstand with her legs bent in the tucked position.

Lunge   *Weight on hands*   *Balance*

1 Molly starts with her arms up in the air and takes a big step forward into a lunge position.

2 She puts her hands on the floor and pushes through her front leg while kicking up her back leg.

3 Squeezing the floor with her fingers helps Molly balance on her hands for longer.

The handstand

Molly can do the handstand without anybody helping her. She has been practicing a lot and now she can stay up in the handstand for a long time.

The Cartwheel

Once you can do a handstand, you are ready to learn how to do a cartwheel. This is when you move onto your hands and swing your legs over your head to travel in a straight line. Jessica began learning the cartwheel by doing bunny hops over a bench. When you can do this with straight legs, you are ready to try the movement on the floor. Jessica is excited because she already knows how to do a cartwheel and is eager to show the class what she can do.

Using a bench is a good way to start learning the cartwheel. Jessica puts both hands on the bench and lifts her legs as high as she can over it, keeping them as straight as possible.

How to do a cartwheel

Jessica starts on her right leg and comes down on her left leg. Traveling in a straight line, she moves from foot to hand, to hand to foot.

Lift your leg

1 Jessica starts off with her hands stretched up high and left leg lifted straight in front of her.

Put your hand on the floor

2 Stepping onto her left foot and lifting her right leg, Jessica puts her left hand on the floor.

One-handed

Jessica can even do a cartwheel putting only one hand on the floor. With more practice, she will eventually be able to do a cartwheel without using her hands at all.

"I can do four cartwheels in a row!"
Jessica

Move your weight onto your hand

Land on a bent leg

5 Finally Jessica brings her right leg down and pushes off strongly with her right hand to stand up again.

3 Now Jessica is beginning to move the weight of her body onto her hands and kick her leg straight up above.

4 Midway through the cartwheel, Jessica is in a split handstand position. Both hands are on the floor and her legs are wide apart.

21

Tiggy stretches her arms and legs out to make a symmetrical star shape. Try to remember to keep your fingers together as you stretch your fingers and toes.

Jumping and Leaping

The girls love to practice jumping, which is taking off from two feet and landing on two feet, and leaping, which is taking off from one foot and landing on the other. They like to see who can jump the highest, leap the furthest, and make the best shape! There are many different types of jump and leap to learn and many different shapes you can make in the air as you jump. Gymnasts use jumps in their floor exercises as well as on the beam, the bars, and when vaulting.

Turning jumps

After learning to jump on the spot, you can try jumping and turning in the air. First try a quarter turn, then a half turn, and finally a 360-degree full turn jump. Don't worry if you lose your balance to begin with! Try turning in both directions. You will probably find it easier to turn one way than the other.

Stretch your arms up	*Bend your knees*	*Swing your arms*	*Jump and twist*

1 Tyra starts her jump in the stretch position, standing up straight and with her arms above her head.

2 To get as much height in her jump as possible, Tyra bends her knees and swings her arms back in the take-off position.

3 Tyra swings her arms up as she pushes down into the floor ready to jump. She starts to turn her hips and shoulders.

4 Up in the air, Tyra twists her body round to the side and extends through her feet and legs and up through her arms.

Molly almost looks as if she is flying in this split leap.

Pike jump

Tuck jump

Land with feet together

5 Tyra lands with her feet together and her knees bent. You could hurt yourself if you land with straight legs.

" *Each time I leap I try to go further.* "
Molly

Shapes in the air

Bouncing on a trampoline helps the girls to jump really high. The more height they achieve in their jump, the more time they have in the air to make an interesting shape. It's fun trying out lots of different shapes.

W jump

23

The girls help to get everything ready before they start vaulting. The big padded mat is heavy, but landing on it will make sure they don't hurt themselves.

Vaulting

Now it's time to try some vaulting. To begin with, the class use the springboard to practice basic jumps onto the vaulting horse and off again. Once they have begun to do this easily, they can learn how to vault using only their hands on the horse. Eventually, with a lot of practice, they may be able to perform difficult vaults with twists and turns in the air.

Learning to bounce

Molly practices little jumps on the springboard so that she bounces like a ball, keeping her legs as straight as possible.

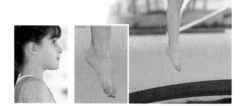

Using the springboard

The first thing to learn in vaulting is the run-up and jump from the springboard. To bounce up high, you need a good, fast run-up, lifting your knees and running on your toes. Then do a hurdle step so that your feet land together on the springiest part of the board (about 8 inches away from the raised end). The higher your take-off, the better your vault will be.

Taking off	*Jumping*	*Landing*

1 Feet together on the springboard, Jessica circles her arms behind her in preparation for her take-off.

2 Jessica stretches her whole body as she flies upwards in the air. Even her fingers and toes are stretched.

3 Keeping her feet together, Jessica bends her knees and ankles to land safely before standing up straight.

1 Squat on

2 Straddle off

The catspring vault is one of the first vaults you will learn. Jessica jumps into a squat onto the horse. Then she moves her hands to the end and straddle vaults off.

Clearing the horse

The vaulting horse is turned sideways for the straddle vault. Tyra jumps off the springboard and reaches forward. She places her hands on the horse so she can push off again to leapfrog over it. She focuses on lifting her legs high enough and wide enough to clear the horse, and then closes them as she leaves the horse.

Catspring vault

Each section of the vaulting horse is hollow inside. The girls like sitting in an unused section while they wait for their turn to vault.

The vaulting horse

The class are using a box vaulting horse, which is made up in sections so you can alter the height depending on the size of the gymnast. The top part of the horse is covered with a nonslip material.

Balancing on the Beam

Being able to perform exercises on the beam, which is only 4 inches wide, takes a lot of practice, confidence, and a good sense of balance. You will always practice skills on the floor first before attempting them on the low beam, then on the high beam. The high beam is surrounded by padded safety mats, in case the gymnasts fall off. To begin with, the class practices walking along the beam gracefully and trying not to wobble. When they have gained more confidence, they can try some more difficult exercises.

Dip step

Jessica can't help looking down as she stands on the beam on one bent leg and dips her other leg down. Tyra is more confident and keeps her head up high and looks straight ahead.

Getting on the beam

There are lots of different ways of getting on the beam at the beginning of your beam exercise. Often a springboard is used to help you jump up and mount the beam either to the side of the beam or at the end.

1 Molly stands to the side of the beam and places her hands flat on top of it.

2 Next she uses her arms and legs to push herself up into the straddle position.

3 With her legs still in the straddle position, Molly turns her body around to the side.

Even though there are safety mats, it can take courage to get on a beam for the first time.

4 Molly completes the mount in the straddle sit position. To dismount, you can jump or somersault or do a handstand off the beam.

" I'm trying hard not to wobble! "
Tiggy

Standing on one leg
with her hands on her
hips helps Hannah
learn balance and
control on the beam.

Jessica, Tiggy, and
Tyra walk along
the beam on tiptoe,
slowly at first.
They are using
their arms to help
them balance.

Chalking up

Gymnasts make sure their hands are well covered with chalk before swinging on the bars. The chalk stops your hands from sweating and slipping when you swing.

Asymmetric Bars

This is the first time that Jessica has been on the bars and she is excited about learning how to swing on them. There are two bars, one higher than the other, some distance apart. Jessica will learn to swing on the low bar first. Tyra has had more practice and can jump from one bar to the other and perform different swinging and circle movements.

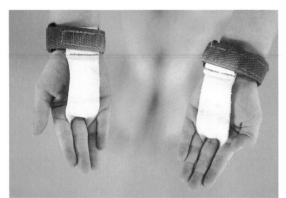

Handguards

These are worn on either one finger or two depending on the size of your hands, to protect the palms of your hands from getting blisters. It's important that they fit well and are not too bulky to affect your grip.

Katie helps lift Jessica up into the front support position on the low bar.

Swing back   **Swing forward**

Front swing to dish

For any swing, you will learn how to control your movement and to think about the shape you make with your body while you swing. It is better to start off with small swings that are easier to control.

1 Katie supports Jessica's wrists as she hangs down from the bar and starts to swing her body back. Jessica tries to keep her shoulders relaxed.

2 Jessica swings her legs forward and *curves* her body into the dish shape at the height of her swing.

2 *Pushing on the bar with her feet and pulling on her hands, Tyra swings her body in a circle backward.*

3 *Tyra takes her feet off the bar, brings her legs together, and extends her body before letting go.*

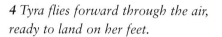

4 *Tyra flies forward through the air, ready to land on her feet.*

Dismounting

There are various ways of getting off the bars. Tyra is practicing a dismount called the straddle on undershoot.

" *Watch me swing off the bars!* **"**
Tyra

Katie helps Tyra balance in the straddle position standing on the bars.

29

Moving Up

Sarah gives each member of the class their Gym Skills certificate. She is really pleased with how hard they have all worked.

This is an exciting day for Jessica and her classmates. Sarah, their coach, has been watching the girls carefully for the past few months to see how well they are performing their moves and if they can do them correctly. The good news is that they have all mastered the basic skills and will receive their certificates!

Jump

The Somersault

A somersault is where you turn head over heels in the air. It can be made forward or backward, and with different shapes. Molly is learning how to do a front tucked somersault. Sarah supports her while she turns in the air. This support is called spotting and allows Molly to try a new skill safely and feel the movement as a whole.

Turn   **Tuck**   **Land**

1 Using the springboard helps Molly to get enough height in her jump to perform the somersault.

2 Up in the air, Sarah helps Molly turn her body, bring her head down, and lift her hips up.

3 Over she goes! Molly brings her knees into her chest to make a tight tucked position.

4 Upright now, Molly straightens her body but bends her knees ready for landing on two feet.

The Foam Pit

Practicing more difficult skills like the somersault is made easier and safer by first trying them with the foam pit to land in. And it's a lot of fun, too!

Conditioning

Now that they have learned the basic skills, the class will spend even more time on their warm-up and conditioning. Molly can now climb the rope with her legs in the straddle position using only her arms to pull herself up.

66 *Gymnastics is really great for making friends.* **99**
Tiggy

Tiggy helps Tyra with her sit-ups by holding Tyra's feet. Only a few more to go and then it will be Tiggy's turn.

Floor Sequence

The class can't wait to watch Issy's performance. They will learn what it is possible to do with hard work and practice.

When you have learned

some basic gymnastics skills, you will be taught how to make a sequence by linking some of the skills together. Issy is in the girls' squad, which means she trains every day and represents the club in competitions. The class are thrilled that she has come to show them her floor routine which, with its series of tumbles and leaps, is breathtaking to watch.

Some of Issy's floor routine is slow and graceful and she can make beautiful shapes with her body.

Here, Issy demonstrates her well-controlled balance and then some fun dance steps.

Issy finishes her routine on bended knee, arms outstretched and smiling.

Floor performance

Dance is an important part of Issy's training. Her floor exercises are performed to music and she must express the mood of the music through her movement. Dance training also helps Issy to make all her moves as fluent and elegant as possible.

This part of the routine is fast and energetic. In her tumble run across the floor, Issy includes a handspring and a backflip at great speed.

Jessica's turn

The class have been inspired by Issy's performance and can't wait to practice some moves themselves. Issy helps Jessica try a backward walkover. When Jessica can do this well, she will be able to use it in her own floor sequence.

To support Jessica properly, Issy stands to the side and makes sure that her hand is firmly in the middle of Jessica's back.

Advanced Beam

Issy shows the other girls how she does the forward splits on the beam.

Issy is staying on a bit longer to show the girls some of the more advanced skills she can do on the beam and to help them with the skills they are learning. In competition on the beam, just like her floor routine, Issy must perform a 70 to 90 second sequence of balances, jumps, and turns that flow easily from one to the other.

Forward roll on the beam

Tyra can do a forward roll easily on the floor. Doing it on the high beam is much harder, but Tyra manages it without falling off.

Tick-Tock sequence

One of the moves Issy performs in her beam routine is a half forward walkover followed by a back walkover. It's called a Tick-Tock because you move your legs first one way, then the other, like the pendulum on a grandfather clock.

Lift up one leg   **Split handstand**   **Split bridge position**

Issy's starting position shows good posture with her arms outstretched and right leg forward.

1 Issy puts both hands on the beam and lifts her right leg high up behind her.

2 Moving forward onto her hands, she kicks her legs into a split handstand position.

3 She brings her right leg over her head to touch the beam, keeping the left leg up straight.

Straddle mount press to handstand

Issy starts her beam exercise with an impressive mount.

Tiggy's turn

Now it's Tiggy's turn to try the handstand on the low beam. Issy supports Tiggy's legs when she has kicked to handstand. When Tiggy has gained confidence on the low beam, she can try it on the high beam.

Supporting

Split handstand

4 *Kicking up with her legs and pushing with her hands, Issy moves back into the split handstand position.*

Lower left leg

5 *Issy slowly lowers her left leg back down to the position she held in step one.*

Stand up straight

6 *Issy is back where she started, having completed a Tick-Tock. Good job, Issy!*

35

Thomas and Miles have to perform two sets of 20 pressups each. This makes their arms stronger so they can lift themselves on the apparatus.

Boys' Apparatus

Thomas and Miles are in the boys' squad. Many of the skills they learn are the same as the girls, and both boys and girls must possess the same qualities of strength, flexibility, and coordination. But in artistic gymnastics, the boys learn to perform on different pieces of apparatus. Instead of the beam and the asymmetric bars, they use the pommel horse, rings, long horse, parallel bars, and the high bar.

1 The boys begin their routine demonstrating good posture as they stand up straight.

Warm-up

For the apparatus the boys will be working on, strength and body control are vitally important. To help them build up their muscles, the boys' warm-up includes a lot of conditioning exercises. It also includes a floor routine with sticks that is designed to strengthen their arm muscles, increase the suppleness in their shoulders, and increase their flexibility.

2 Having picked up the sticks, the boys lift them up straight in front of them.

3 Now they lean forward, and bring their arms straight up above their head.

4 Keeping their arms straight, they bring the sticks behind their back and stand up.

Floor exercises

Floor exercises are performed by both girls and boys. Although they do not perform their exercises to music like the girls, the boys must be able to move gracefully and artistically.

A bucket suspended from the roof on a piece of rope helps Miles to practice his circling technique! Miles can concentrate on his arms while his legs are supported by the bucket.

"I can do 10 circles!"
Thomas

The pommel horse
At nine years old, Thomas has only just started working on this piece of apparatus, as it requires great strength and concentration. Eventually, he will learn how to balance on one hand while swinging his legs around the handles.

The mushroom
Before the boys learn to use the pommel horse, they practice circling their legs around the mushroom.

Chalk up

Thomas and Miles rub the chalk onto their hands so that they can get a good grip on the rings and the bars.

Rings and Bars

The boys need great strength to work on these two pieces of apparatus. Of the two, the rings are perhaps the most difficult. The boys must learn how to get into certain positions and hold them still. When they have mastered these static holds, they will learn to swing from one position to another without touching the rope or rings with their body. On the parallel bars, the boys learn how to swing themselves into different positions above and below the bars. To do this they need strength, technique, and balance.

Muscle up

When you first start exercises on the rings, your coach will help you up. The muscles in Thomas' arms are now developed enough for him to lift himself up on his own.

Thomas gets ready to train on the rings.

Muscle up

Push down

Hang on

1 Thomas grips the rings firmly, keeps his shoulders back, and bends his arms behind him. He keeps his head up and looks straight ahead.

2 Pushing down on the rings, Thomas is able to lift himself up into the front support position using only the strength in his arms.

3 Hanging upside down, Thomas concentrates on making his body as straight as he can, stretching his legs, feet and toes.

Thomas practices a handstand on the parallets before trying it on the parallel bars.

Lift your legs

Swing back

Swing to handstand

For this exercise, you need strength, control, and balance.

1 *From the half lever position, Thomas must swing his hips forward to gain momentum for his backward swing.*

2 *Now Thomas swings his body back and up into a handstand and holds it as steady as he can.*

" I can do a half lever. "
Miles

Miles is learning to stretch his legs straight out in front of him and to keep as still as he can.

Give me five

At the end of the class, Thomas and Miles congratulate themselves. They have worked really hard.

Molly hopes that the judges will like the routine she is learning on the asymmetric bars.

" *I just want to do my best.* "
Tyra

Preparing *for the* Championship

A*t the end of year,* a championship competition is held for all the children in the gymnastics school to take part in. Everyone is very excited and working hard to prepare their routines on the different pieces of apparatus. They all want to put on their best performance!

Performing

You may feel nervous before taking part in a competition or performing in front of other people. The important thing is to do your best and enjoy yourself. Don't worry if you make a mistake—just carry on with the routine. If you look confident and happy, then the audience will feel happy and confident, too.

Sarah helps Jessica steady herself on the beam as she practices an arabesque. Jessica hopes she can do it on the day without wobbling.

Hannah's floor routine

Most gymnasts find that there is one piece of apparatus that they like to work on best. Hannah enjoys all the apparatus but her favorite excercise is the floor routine. She likes being able to perform skills to music.

Vault practice

Tiggy practices a handspring vault on the mat. She will get judged on her take-off and landing as well as on the handspring itself.

Arabesque

It works! Jessica remembers the advice her coach gave her about balancing and she keeps her eyes fixed straight ahead. Slowly, she lifts her leg behind her—and doesn't wobble. What an amazing achievement!

Championship

A*t last the* day of the championship has arrived. The children have new leotards to wear on this special day and are ready to take part in the competition. They have all worked hard, and everyone's a winner.

" *This has been the best day of my life!* **"**
Jessica

The hard work Molly put into preparing for the championships has paid off. She has done really well on all the apparatus.

Tyra felt a bit nervous before the championship began, but her nerves soon disappeared when she started her routines. What a star!

Hannah has been looking forward to showing her family all the things she has learned to do in gymnastics. And she can't wait to show them her medal.

The boys' championship

The boys have to perform on two more pieces of apparatus than the girls and their routines are a little longer. Thomas and Miles have both given medal-winning performances. It's been an amazing day!

Hannah   *Jessica*   *Tyra*

" *One day I might be in the Olympics.* "
Hannah

Tiggy

Molly and Issy

Thomas and Miles

Olympic dreams!

Everyone dreams about what
they could do in the future.
These promising young gymnasts
will keep practicing their sport
because they love it. If they are
good enough, they might even
make it into the Olympic team.
What a great dream to have!

Glossary

A

Apparatus—the equipment used in gymnastics.
Arch—a body shape made by lying on your stomach and lifting your arms and legs.
Asymmetric bars—two bars, one higher than the other, some distance apart.

B

Beam—a plank of wood 15 feet long and 4 inches wide for performing balance skills.
Bridge—a body shape made with the feet and hands on the floor and the back pushed up to form a bridge.

C

Cartwheel—a turning move performed on your hands with your legs swinging over your head.
Catspring—a vault consisting of a squat on jump onto the horse and leapfrog off it.

D

Dish—a body shape made by lying on your back and lifting your arms and legs.

H

Handguards—guards to protect your hands from blisters when you are on the bars.
Handstand—balancing on your hands with your legs straight up in the air.
Headstand—balancing on your head and hands with your legs straight up in the air.

L

Lumberfold—bending forward at the waist so that your chest touches your legs.

P

Parallel bars—two bars of the same height and only a small distance apart.
Parallets—parallel bars on the floor.
Pike—a V-shaped position where you stretch your legs out straight in front and try to touch your toes.
Pommel horse—a vaulting horse with two handles fitted on the top.

S

Somersault—turning head over heels in the air.
Split handstand—a handstand position with your legs in the splits.
Splits—when you stretch your legs out either side of you or one leg in front and one behind.
Straddle—a position with your legs stretched out to either side.

T

Tuck—a position with your knees brought up to your chest.

V

Vaulting horse—apparatus used by girls and boys for performing vaults and leaps.

Acknowledgments

Dorling Kindersley would like to thank the following for their help in the preparation and production of this book:

Heathrow Gymnastics Club, Green Lane, Hounslow, Middlesex, TW4 6DH (www.heathrowgymnastics.org.uk), for their kind permission to photograph the book there.

Special thanks to Vincent Walduck for acting as consultant and coaches Sarah Fiander, Katie Cannon and John Dalglish who were so good with the children; all the gymnasts and their parents; Michele Walduck; Kate Simkins; Patsy Burrell for the beautiful handmade leotards; photographer David Handley and photography assistant Rob Mason.

Index

A

Arabesque 41, 42
Arch 14
Asymmetric bars 28

B

Backward roll 17
Backward walkover 33
Beam 26, 34, 40, 41, 42
Box splits 13
Bridge 14,15

C

Cartwheel 20, 21
Catspring vault 25
Conditioning 14, 31, 36

D

Dip step 26
Dish 14, 28

F

Floor sequence 32
Foam pit 30
Forward roll 16, 17, 34
Front support 14, 28, 38

H

Half lever 39
Handguards 28
Handspring 33, 41
Handstands 19, 35
Headstands 18

J

Japana 11
Jumping 22, 23

L

Leaping 22, 23
Leg lifts 14
Lumberfold 11

M

Mushroom 37

P

Parallel bars 39
Parallets 39
Pike 23
Pommel horse 37
Press-ups 36

R

Rings 38
Rope climbing 14, 31

S

Sit-ups 31
Somersault 30, 31
Split handstand 34, 35
Splits 12, 13, 34
Springboard 17, 24, 30
Straddle 17, 25, 26, 29, 31, 35
Straddle lever 11
Stretching 10, 11

T

Tick-Tock 34
Tuck 8, 23

V

Vaulting 24, 25
Vaulting horse 25

W

Wall bars 14
Warm-up 8, 9, 31, 36
W-jump 23